Know your Rules

Copyright © 2006 by Kristi C. Love Collection

All rights Reserved. No part of this publication may be reproduced or transmitted by any means, electronic, mechanical, or otherwise, including photocopying and recording, or by any information storage or retrieval system, without permission - in writing - from the publishers.

Library of Congress Catalog number:

Kristi Colvin-Williams
First Edition: Kristofer Says Know Your Rules
SAN:
SBN: ISBN: 0-9777022-1-9
Illustrations by Massive Brain

Edited by: A Mother's love Publishing,
Black Jack, Missouri 63033 • http://www.kristiclovecol.com

Know

Kristofer Say's

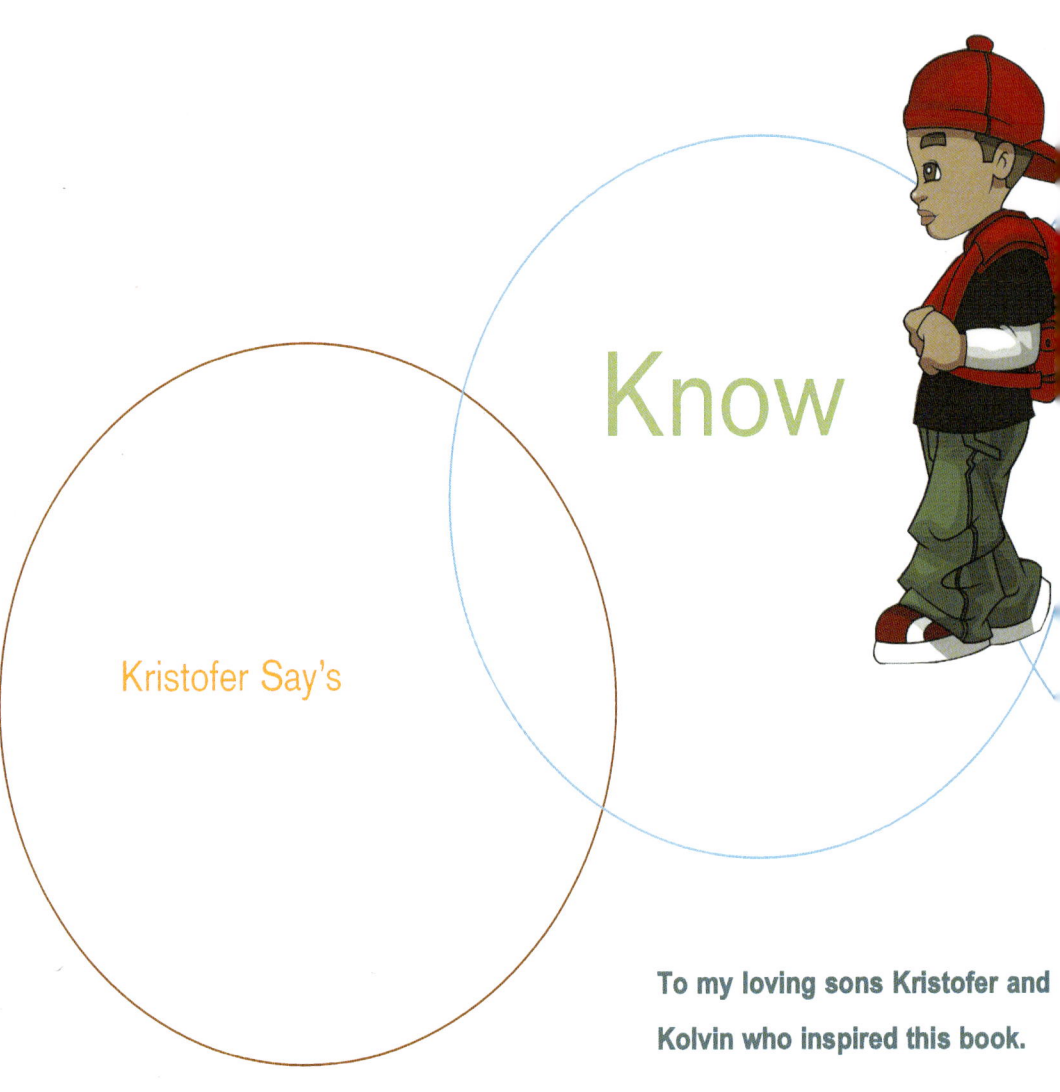

To my loving sons Kristofer and Kolvin who inspired this book.

Rules

your

Words to Know

A
A, An, As, At, All, And, Any, Are, Art, Also, A lot, Away, Asleep, About, After
Asked, Again, Answer, Adults, Anyone, Anyway, August, Awaken, Around, Awesome, Arrived, Anytime, Already, Anything, Anywhere

E
Eat, End, Easy, Even, Eager, Early, Eating
Empty, Entire, Everyone, Exciting, Expected, Explained

I
I, If, Is, It, It's
Idea, Imagine, Imagined, Important

B
Be, By, Bell, Big, Bus, Boy's
Before, Bright, Broken, Become, Because, Breakfast

F
For, Fast, Feel, From, Food, Full, Feast
First, Foods, Family, Follow, Favorite, Friendly

J
Just

C
Can, Come, Class, Could, Crazy, Crumb
Crunchy, Couldn't, Children, Crawling, Classroom, Computers

G
Go, Get, Gym, Glad, Gone
Good, Going, Good-bye, Great, Growl

K
Kids, know, Kolvin, Kristofer, Kindergarten

H
He, Had, Has, Him, His, Hot, How, Hand, Have, Help
Home, Hour, Hands, Happy, Happen, Having, Hungry, Hall, Heading

L
Lots, Let's, Like, Loud, Learn
Lunch, Lesson, Learned, Leaving, Lunchroom

D
Do, Dad, Day, Does
Down, Didn't, Dangerous

4

M
May
Met
Mid
Made
Many
Meal
Mean
Mess
More
Most

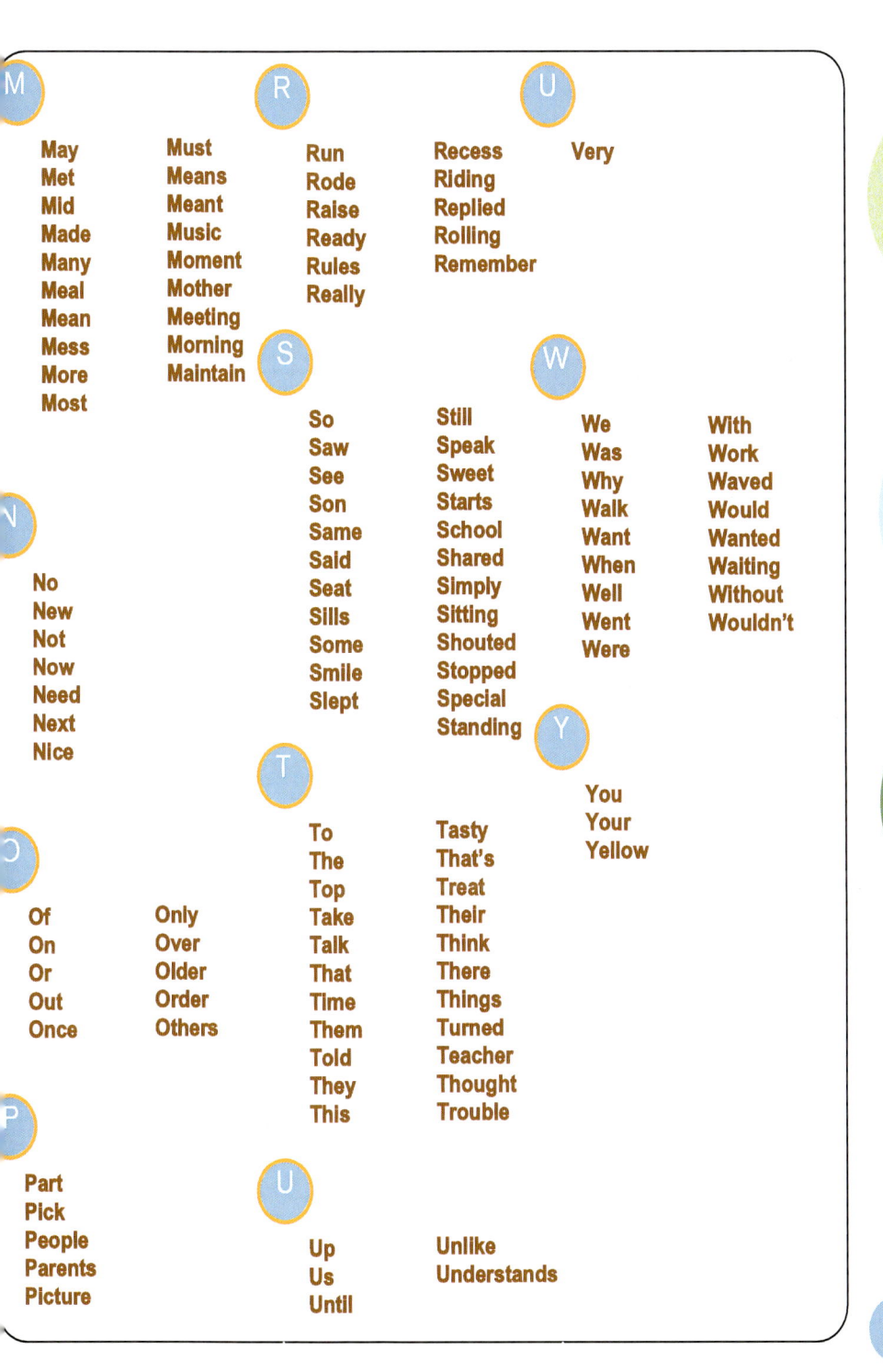

Must
Means
Meant
Music
Moment
Mother
Meeting
Morning
Maintain

N
No
New
Not
Now
Need
Next
Nice

O
Of
On
Or
Out
Once

Only
Over
Older
Order
Others

P
Part
Pick
People
Parents
Picture

R
Run
Rode
Raise
Ready
Rules
Really

Recess
Riding
Replied
Rolling
Remember

S
So
Saw
See
Son
Same
Said
Seat
Sills
Some
Smile
Slept

Still
Speak
Sweet
Starts
School
Shared
Simply
Sitting
Shouted
Stopped
Special
Standing

T
To
The
Top
Take
Talk
That
Time
Them
Told
They
This

Tasty
That's
Treat
Their
Think
There
Things
Turned
Teacher
Thought
Trouble

U
Up
Us
Until

Unlike
Understands

Very

W
We
Was
Why
Walk
Want
When
Well
Went
Were

With
Work
Waved
Would
Wanted
Waiting
Without
Wouldn't

Y
You
Your
Yellow

It was a bright mid August morning.
This was a very special day for Kristofer and Kolvin. It was their first day of school. Kristofer was awake and ready an hour before the bus was to come.

Unlike Kristofer, Kolvin was still fast asleep. Kolvin slept until he was awakened by his mother.

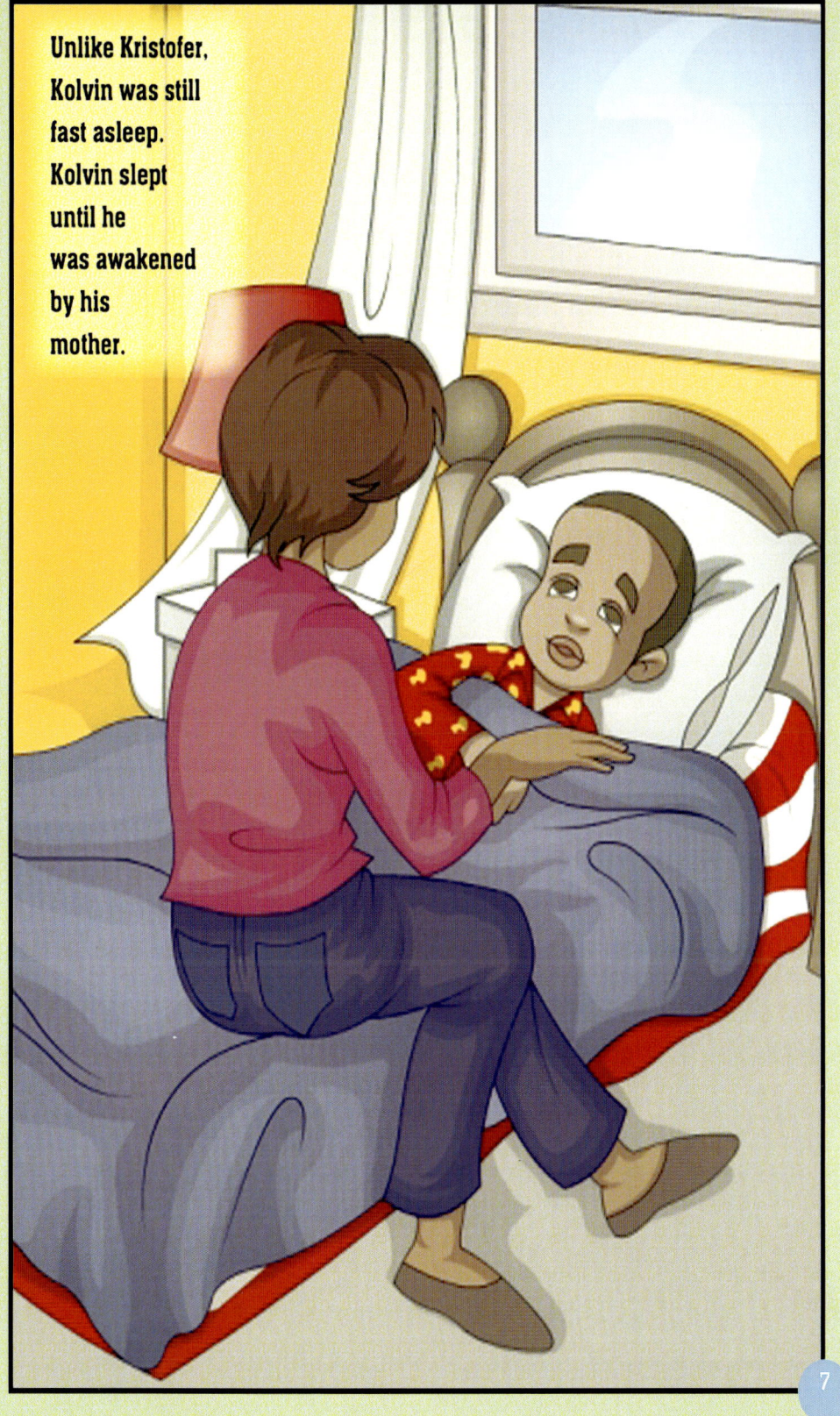

Before heading out for work and school the family shared breakfast, the most important meal of the day.

When the bus arrived at school it was just as they had imagined, a big school with a lot of friendly people.

Mr. Wise was the boy's teacher. He waited for each student to arrive at school before he explained all of the school rules. He wrote each rule on the board before the students went to their other classes.

NO CANDY OR GUM
NO TALKING
NO TOYS

Meeting all of their new teachers and going to recess was really fun, but the school day had come to an end. The first day was now over.

On the walk home their dad asked the boys about their big day at school.
"It was great! I met a lot of new people and learned some new things," Kristofer replied.
"It's just ..."
"It's just what?" asked their dad.
"Well dad, why do we have so many rules?" Kristofer asked.

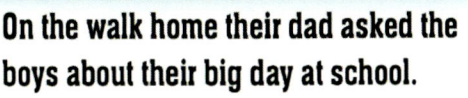

Discussion Questions

What was the story about?
- (A) being late to class
- (B) playing soccer
- (C) following rules

Why do we need rules?
- (A) to be mean
- (B) to keep order
- (C) to eat lunch

How would school be without rules?
- (A) school would be a big mess
- (B) it ran smoothly
- (C) school was the same

Discuss the importance of following rules.

What was the name of the classes Kristofer attended?
- (A) recess, lunch, gym
- (B) math, art, recess
- (C) music, art, gym

Discussion Questions

What meal did the family share?

- A. breakfast
- B. lunch
- C. dinner

Who were the boys happy to see?

- A. Mr. Wise
- B. their dad
- C. the lunch lady

Who in the story was awake and ready an hour before the bus was to come?

- A. Kristofer
- B. Kolvin
- C. their Dad

In one sentence, write something you have learned from this story?